WILT CHAMBERLAIN

Read all of the books in this exciting, action-packed biography series!

Alex Rodriguez	Muhammad Ali
Annika Sorenstam	Pelé
Barry Bonds	Peyton Manning
Cal Ripken Jr.	Roberto Clemente
David Beckham	Sandy Koufax
Derek Jeter	Sasha Cohen
Doug Flutie	Tiger Woods
Hank Aaron	Tim Duncan
Ichiro Suzuki	Tom Brady
Jesse Owens	Tony Dungy
Jim Thorpe	Wayne Gretzky
Joe DiMaggio	Willie Mays
Josh Gibson	Wilma Rudolph
Lance Armstrong	Wilt Chamberlain
Michelle Kwan	Yao Ming
Mickey Mantle	

WILT CHAMBERLAIN

by Matt Doeden

Twenty-First Century Books/Minneapolis

For my Grandpa and Grandma Doeden.
I wish I'd had a chance to know you both.

Twenty-First Century Books
A division of Lerner Publishing Group, Inc.
241 First Avenue North
Minneapolis, MN 55401 U.S.A.

Website address: www.lernerbooks.com

Front cover: © Focus on Sport/Getty Images.
Back cover: © iStockphoto.com/Bill Grove.

Library of Congress Cataloging-in-Publication Data

Doeden, Matt.
    Wilt Chamberlain / by Matt Doeden.
       p.   cm. — (Sports heroes and legends)
    Includes bibliographical references and index.
    ISBN 978–0–7613–5369–0 (lib. bdg. : alk. paper)
    1. Chamberlain, Wilt, 1936–1999– —Juvenile literature. 2. Basketball players—United States—Biography—Juvenile literature. 3. African American basketball players—Biography—Juvenile literature. I. Title.
GV884.C5D65 2011
796.323092—dc22 [B]   2010000890

Manufactured in the United States of America
1 — VI — 7/15/10

Contents

Prologue

One Hundred

During the 1961–1962 National Basketball Association (NBA) season, Wilt Chamberlain of the Philadelphia Warriors was doing things that almost defied belief. By March 2, 1962, the 7-foot-1 center had already scored 60 or more points in a game a jaw-dropping seventeen times. In one of those games, he'd netted 78 points against the Los Angeles Lakers for a single-game NBA scoring record.

Wilt was about to make 78 look paltry. He and the Philadelphia Warriors were in Hershey, Pennsylvania, to host a late-season game against the New York Knicks. The game was all but meaningless in the NBA standings. The Warriors had already clinched a playoff berth, while the Knicks were out of the playoff chase. Only 4,124 people bothered showing up. The game wasn't even televised. Nobody could have known that this otherwise unimportant game would become one of the most memorable in NBA history.

The Knicks' starting center, Phil Jordan, was out with an injury. That left backup Darrall Imhoff with the primary duty of guarding Wilt. It was clear early on that the Knicks were outmatched. The Warriors jumped out to an early 19–3 lead, with Wilt scoring 13 of their points. That was nothing unusual, though. Wilt was averaging 50 points a night. Even when he finished the first quarter with 23 points, few eyebrows were raised.

The Knicks fought back in the second quarter. They tried to clamp down on Wilt in hopes of keeping the game close, but with little success. By halftime Wilt had 41 points and the Warriors were ahead 79–68. It was a comfortable lead, but the game was still in doubt. In the locker room, Philly coach Frank McGuire told his team to keep giving the ball to the big man.

The Knicks knew what the Warriors' second-half strategy would be. They devoted two, three, and sometimes four men to stopping Wilt. But even that wasn't enough. They tried fouling Wilt, hacking at his arms, trying to throw him off his game. The tactic failed. All it did was make Wilt mad. He scored 28 points in the third quarter and propelled the Warriors to a 21-point lead. After three quarters, Wilt had 69 points and was well on his way to breaking his own record of 78 in a game.

Imhoff fouled out in the fourth quarter, removing what little resistance the Knicks had to Wilt's onslaught. Imhoff would later take the blame for letting Wilt score so many points. But Wilt pointed out that New York's backup center was the only thing keeping him remotely in check. "He played me as well as anyone. He fouled out in the fourth quarter, and that's when I really started getting points. He was no more at fault than anyone."

By this time, the Knicks had abandoned all hopes of winning. They had only one goal in mind: to stop Wilt from embarrassing them. The NBA had no shot clock at the time. That meant teams could run down the clock by holding on to the ball for long periods. Despite trailing by more than 20 points, the Knicks chose that tactic. The Warriors countered the Knicks' strategy by fouling and forcing a fast pace. The Warriors did everything they could to help Wilt score again and again. Guard Al Attles passed on an easy layup at one point just so he could get the ball to Wilt for another two points.

Wilt broke his own scoring record with almost eight minutes left to play. Then he had a new goal: 100 points. By this time, the game had stopped resembling a normal basketball game. The Warriors did everything they could to help Wilt reach 100 points. In turn, the Knicks would foul anyone but Wilt, letting the Warriors' other players take free throws just to keep Wilt from scoring.

"They were willing to do anything to stop me," Wilt said.

With two and a half minutes to play, Wilt had 92 points. The Warriors had the ball, and Wilt took his position in the low block (the area near the basket). Knicks surrounded him on all sides, but teammate Guy Rodgers threw the ball to Wilt anyway. Because Wilt had a 5-inch height advantage on the tallest remaining Knicks, they could not deny him the ball. Wilt caught it, rose up, and hit a fade-away shot off the backboard and through the hoop—94 points. A layup soon after extended his record to 96.

The crowd was buzzing. They chanted for the Warriors to "Give it to Wilt!" They had nothing to worry about—the Philadelphia players had no intention of doing anything else. Guard York Larese sprinted the ball up the court. As he approached the basket, he heard Wilt running behind him. Larese threw up an arcing lob pass. In one fluid motion, Wilt caught the pass and rammed home a rim-rattling dunk—points 97 and 98.

Just over a minute remained. But rather than run down the court to set up the Philly defense, Wilt turned to where the Knicks were inbounding the ball. He reached up and stole the pass. Quickly, he launched a shot from near the free-throw line. The ball caught the rim and rolled around before spinning out. Wilt was still at 98 points.

The Knicks made one free throw, then the Warriors had the ball again. Rodgers knew that the Knicks would foul someone to prevent Wilt from getting the ball. So he didn't give them the chance. He heaved a long pass down the court to Wilt, who jumped high to grab it. Wilt put up another quick shot, but once again he missed. New York was paying so much attention to him, however, that Philly's Ted Luckenbill grabbed the rebound. He threw it to Wilt, and Wilt missed again. The crowd was getting restless.

Luckenbill once again grabbed the rebound. He threw it out to Warriors guard Joe Ruklick. The Knicks charged, intending to foul Ruklick. But before they could reach him, the guard heaved a high pass toward the basket. Wilt rose above the rim to catch the ball. This time, he didn't miss the shot. He slammed it through the rim—100 points! The arena exploded with excitement.

Spectators rushed onto the court and mobbed Wilt with congratulations. Nine minutes later, the court had finally been cleared for the game's meaningless final 46 seconds. When the final buzzer sounded, the Warriors had a 169–147 victory (which set a record for the most combined points in an NBA game), and Wilt had done something almost unthinkable. He'd scored 100 points in an NBA game.

Wilt's feat would become the stuff of legend, but he always insisted that his teammates had as much to do with his record as he did. "[They went] way beyond the call of duty," Wilt said. "They were so clever finding ways to get me the ball. They had to do more than just give up open shots. They had to avoid fouls and pass me the ball in traffic."

Wilt's 100-point night was just one of his amazing accomplishments in the NBA. And like much of what Wilt did on the basketball court, that feat is unlikely ever to be matched.

Chapter | One

A Growing Star

The baby boy born to William and Olivia Chamberlain on August 21, 1936, in Philadelphia, Pennsylvania, didn't seem out of the ordinary. Little Wilton Norman Chamberlain weighed 8 pounds, 10 ounces and was 22 inches long—a perfectly normal size for a healthy baby. Little Wilt's parents both stood under 6 feet tall themselves. Nothing about Wilt hinted that he'd one day grow to be a giant of a man—and a giant of a star.

Wilt was the fifth of nine children in the Chamberlain family (William and Olivia also had had two children who did not survive infancy.) He had two brothers and six sisters. His father worked as a janitor for a publishing company and as a part-time handyman, while his mother worked as a housekeeper. She also took charge of her nine children, and Wilt later admitted that his mother was the only person in the world whom he feared.

The Chamberlain home was a gathering place for many neighborhood kids. Between siblings and friends, young Wilt never lacked for playmates. But soon he realized he was different from the other children. He was growing at a shocking rate. By the age of 10, at 6 feet tall, he already towered over both of his parents.

A FASHION STATEMENT

As a kid, Wilt used to wear rubber bands on his long legs to keep his socks up. He kept a supply of rubber bands on his wrist, both on and off the court. He continued the habit in adulthood. He claimed that the rubber bands helped remind him of where he'd come from.

Wilt, like all his siblings, worked for his spending money and to help bring money into the household. He had all sorts of jobs, from a newspaper route to yard work to a job in a candy store. From an early age, Wilt's parents instilled in him a strong work ethic. They made sure he understood that nothing came for free and that he had to work for what he wanted in life. It was a lesson that would serve Wilt well in adulthood.

"It wasn't that I had to work," he later said. "My family wasn't rich, but it wasn't poor either. I just wanted to have a nickel or dime in my pocket to spend, as I wished to be different from the other kids."

Wilt's competitive nature set him apart as well. His family never pushed sports on him. His mother had no interest in sports at all, and his dad's interest in sports stretched no further than boxing. Regardless, Wilt was confident and aggressive while playing sports or games. He hated to lose and wasn't above cheating at a card game to push the odds in his favor.

As outgoing as Wilt may have been in competition, in social situations he was often shy and reserved. He was likely self-conscious about a stutter in his speech, and he was also a slow learner in school, needing special reading classes. The school even held him back a grade one year. It wasn't that Wilt wasn't smart. Those who knew him insisted that he was bright and focused. He just learned a little more slowly early on.

Athletics was a way for Wilt to assert and express himself. His size may have made him different in social situations, but it gave him a much-needed shot of confidence in sports. Despite his height advantage, young Wilt didn't really like basketball much. He preferred track and field. His long legs made him a fast runner.

But soon basketball became central to Wilt's life. The choice was probably inevitable, considering Wilt's imposing height and that basketball was the game of choice among most of the kids in his neighborhood. They played basketball at a local recreation center and on several recreational and community teams. Because of his size, Wilt often played with boys much older than he was.

By the age of thirteen, Wilt had decided that he wanted to be a professional basketball player. He starred on the Shoemaker Junior High School team in Philadelphia. In high school, Wilt was a true force on the basketball court. He attended Overbrook High School, which was renowned for its powerful basketball program. Overbrook's student population was mostly white, but Wilt didn't face much racism. Most of the white students were Jewish. They knew what prejudice felt like. Perhaps that shared knowledge helped Overbrook students avoid the racial tension that plagued many racially mixed schools during that time period.

Wilt kept getting better. In 1953 he led his YMCA community team to a national title at a tournament in North Carolina. That year he was a sophomore at Overbrook. He averaged 31 points per game and led Overbrook to the Public League title game. He also earned the nickname Wilt the Stilt. Wilt hated the nickname, but it would stick with him for the rest of his life.

THE BIG DIPPER

As a teen, Wilt got the nickname the Big Dipper, or Dippy, because of the way he had to dip his head below the door frame when entering or exiting a room.

In the Public League title game, Overbrook faced off against Northeast High School, led by future NBA player Guy Rodgers. Rodgers scored 26 points in the game. But Wilt did even better, scoring 34 and getting the victory.

Next, Overbrook took on the champions of Philadelphia's Catholic League for the city title. The Catholic League champs, West Philadelphia Catholic High School, devoted three and sometimes four defenders to stopping Wilt. Even though Wilt got 29 points in the game, the strategy worked. Overbrook lost the game 54–42.

Wilt's time in high school wasn't limited to basketball, however. He had become a good student after his struggles in his younger years. He was popular, though he was very shy with girls. He also starred for the school's track team. His long stride and endurance made him an excellent runner, and he could out-jump almost anybody. In fact, he won the Public League high-jump championship in 1953.

Still, it was becoming increasingly clear that Wilt's future was in basketball. His height (6 feet 11 inches when he entered high school) and skill had made him something of a celebrity in Philadelphia. He was noticed even on a national scale. By 1954 Wilt was like a man among boys, scoring at will. While some recognized him as a dominant force, others started to call him a ball hog. His prolific scoring caused some friction with his teammates.

According to Overbrook teammate Doug Leaman, "Me and the other players were trying to score double figures so we could get [college] scholarships, but Wilt [was] scoring 30 and 40 points. . . . It wasn't fun."

Still, the formula won games. Overbrook once again won the Public League title. This time they took things a step further by winning the city title, defeating South Catholic High School 74–50. The title game capped off an amazing 19–0 season.

❝Wilt had three things to overcome: he was tall, he was black, and he had a speech impediment [stutter]. . . . Wilt couldn't hide inside himself. You can't hide when you're 6'11" and 15 years old. That left [emotional] scars on him.❞

—SONNY HILL, WILT'S CHILDHOOD FRIEND

According to many media members and basketball experts, Wilt could have held his own in the NBA in 1954. But he still had a year of high school to go. By his senior season, the name Wilt Chamberlain was famous among basketball fans nationwide. He had his choice of any college in the nation. He stood 7 feet tall. And unlike many very tall youngsters, Wilt was comfortable with his giant frame. He didn't have the clumsiness so common to many young big men. He had skills. He could shoot. He could dribble and handle the ball. And although he didn't use the skill much, he could pass.

Wilt and Overbrook lost only one game during the 1954–1955 season. That season Wilt broke the Pennsylvania high school scoring record with 74 points in a single game. When a player on another team scored 78 points in February, Wilt took it upon himself to get the record back, scoring 90 the very next week.

Overbrook cruised to the city title once again, destroying West Catholic High School 83–42. For the season, Wilt averaged an amazing 47 points per game. Then he moved on to track and field, winning another high-jump title as well as the shot put event. He capped off his high school career by graduating in the spring of 1955.

Meanwhile, the stampede to recruit Wilt was on. More than 120 colleges made him scholarship offers. They practically begged Wilt to attend their schools and play basketball for them. And colleges weren't the only ones applying pressure. At the time, the NBA allowed teams to draft local college stars (those who played for teams within 50 miles of an NBA franchise). So NBA coaches pushed Wilt in one direction or another, knowing that if he attended a nearby college, they would have his territorial rights when he moved to the NBA. Such attention for a high schooler was unprecedented.

"[Wilt] came into high school very humble. By his junior year, he was cocky. . . . He knew he could get anything he wanted and go to any college he wanted."

—MEL BRODSKY, WILT'S HIGH SCHOOL TEAMMATE

Despite all this jockeying, Wilt had his own ideas about his future. He wanted to play outside of a big city like his hometown of Philadelphia. And because of rampant racism in the South, he disregarded all southern schools.

Wilt found the perfect fit in the University of Kansas in Lawrence. The school wasn't within 50 miles of any NBA team. So his territorial rights would stay with Philadelphia. The university had a storied basketball program, and Wilt was impressed by coach Forrest Allen. As a bonus, Kansas had a good track-and-field team. Wilt's future was in basketball, but he still loved track and would compete in both sports.

So the biggest question around college basketball that year was finally answered. Wilt was headed to Lawrence to become a Kansas Jayhawk.

Chapter Two

Kansas Jayhawk

Before the 1955 school year, Wilt packed his things and drove to Kansas. His high school teammate Doug Leaman went along for the ride, having also accepted a scholarship to play for Kansas. But Wilt didn't get the warm reception in his new state that he'd been expecting. The pair stopped in a Kansas diner for some food, but the staff refused to serve Wilt in the main dining area because he was black.

Wilt was furious. He hadn't realized that racism—and segregation—was still alive and well in Kansas. He was almost ready to turn around and go back to Philadelphia. But when Wilt arrived in Lawrence, Coach Allen calmed him down and convinced him to stay. (Leaman, however, did soon return home, never playing a game for the Jayhawks.)

Allen didn't stop at just words either. Allen's son was the county attorney, and he made sure Wilt would never encounter another situation like the one he had faced at the diner. Not that such discrimination would be a problem for Wilt in Lawrence. Wilt Chamberlain was a star there before he ever stepped foot onto the basketball court. No business owner in the city would so much as think of turning him away.

Wilt stayed in a university dormitory and slept in a bed custom-made for his large size. The entire city was eager to see Wilt on the court. At the time, major college teams were split into two units—a freshman team and a varsity team. By rule, freshmen weren't eligible to play for the varsity team. People flocked to the arena to see Wilt's first appearance, on November 18, 1955. It was an exhibition game in which the team's freshmen played the upperclassmen. The younger, less experienced freshmen routinely lost such games, but not this time. Wilt and the freshmen won the game 81–71. Wilt's 42 points and 29 rebounds only added to fans' sense of anticipation, as well as to their frustration that Wilt would have to wait another year to help Kansas seek a national title.

After the 1955–1956 season, Allen retired and Dick Harp took over the program. Wilt was bitter that Allen wouldn't be coaching him, and he never warmed up to Harp. Wilt also seemed disinterested in his academic career. According to a friend, he rarely bothered to attend classes, and he sometimes sent other students to take tests for him. In those days, universities didn't set high standards for student athletes, and Kansas seemed willing to look the other way for its new star. Wilt, meanwhile, focused on his social life. He was no longer the shy, awkward kid he'd been in Philly. He joined a fraternity and frequently went to nearby Kansas City to visit the city's many jazz clubs. All things told, Wilt's freshman year was remarkably unproductive.

Perhaps the most memorable part of Wilt's first year in college came during his time with the track-and-field team. His events included the shot put, the triple jump, and the high jump. It was in the latter that he excelled. That year his best official jump was 6 feet 4.75 inches—a Big Seven Conference indoor record for a freshman.

FLIPPIN' WITH THE DIPPER

Wilt's interests at Kansas weren't limited to sports. For a short time, he hosted his own program on a local radio station. The program, called *Flippin' with the Dipper*, featured some of Wilt's favorite music—mostly blues and jazz.

In his sophomore season, Wilt finally got to join the varsity team. College basketball fans nationwide were eager to see if the man could live up to the hype. The National Collegiate Athletic Association (NCAA) had even changed some rules in anticipation of Wilt's skills. It outlawed offensive goaltending (when an offensive player touches a shot as it travels down toward the rim) and forced players to stay behind the free-throw line on foul shots. Wilt could jump from the free-throw line and dunk his foul shots, a skill that NCAA officials feared would allow him to make every free throw he ever took. An article in the *Saturday Evening Post* even asked the question: "Can basketball survive Wilt Chamberlain?"

Wilt's varsity debut finally came on December 3, 1956, against Northwestern. The twenty-year-old Wilt did not disappoint. He dominated in every way possible. He scored a Kansas-record 52 points and pulled down a shocking 31 rebounds (another record) in an 87–69 victory. In his first game, Wilt had already done more than anyone in Kansas history. His performance was arguably the most impressive college basketball debut the NCAA has ever seen.

"Those fabulous stories about Wilt 'the Stilt' Chamberlain are true," wrote one reporter. "He proved it last night."

Behind Wilt's play, the Jayhawks were the hands-down favorites to win their conference, the Big Seven, and were ranked as the top team in national polls as well. The Jayhawks went on to win their first twelve games of the season before losing 39–37 to Iowa State, which used a defense designed strictly to stop Wilt.

All was not perfect, however. Wilt struggled with his free throws, making just over 60 percent of them. Teams fouled him mercilessly, knowing that was their best chance to slow him down. Free throwing was one rare chink in his armor.

Regardless, Wilt and the Jayhawks were a hot ticket. Average attendance at games increased by more than eight thousand fans per game in his first season. Kansas cruised to the Big Seven Conference title with an 11–1 conference record and earned a trip to the NCAA Tournament. At the time, the tournament featured twenty-three teams split into four regions. The Jayhawks were off to the Midwest regional, which was held in Dallas, Texas.

Traveling to the South presented immediate problems. The hotel Kansas was booked to stay in would not allow black people. Coach Harp refused to separate his team. Instead, the Jayhawks traveled to a hotel in nearby Grand Prairie, Texas.

The racism in Texas was severe. Kansas's first game was against Southern Methodist University (SMU), an all-white team. Members of the crowd threw things at the Kansas players and shouted racial slurs.

SMU was a good team, and center Jim Krebs proved a worthy opponent for Wilt. With about five minutes left in the second half, SMU held a 3-point lead. But Krebs, who had been forced to play very physical defense against Wilt, committed his fifth foul and was out of the game. With Krebs out, SMU had nobody who could match up to Wilt. SMU tried to milk the clock by holding the ball, but Kansas managed to tie the game in the final seconds. In the five-minute overtime, SMU had no chance. Wilt and the Jayhawks claimed a 73–65 victory to advance to the regional championship.

Krebs gave Wilt's game mixed reviews. "I had all the good shots I needed to get my points but I just couldn't hit anything," he said. "Chamberlain is a wonderful offensive player, but I could get all the shots I wanted off him."

The abusive treatment from the crowd continued the next night in the regional title game, against Oklahoma State. But once again, the Jayhawks ignored the racial abuse and won the game, 81–61. Wilt's composure impressed many, including *Sports Illustrated* writers Tex Maule and Jeremiah Tax. They wrote, "Chamberlain, who draws an inordinate number of fouls, took a tremendous amount of booing from the crowd with considerable grace. . . . He plays with a serene assurance unusual in a sophomore, and he does the things he can do so very well that he often appears cocky."

The victory sent Kansas to the Final Four (to be played in Kansas City, Missouri). There they would battle for a national championship. Their first opponent was the University of San Francisco—a team that had won the previous two NCAA titles. San Francisco was no match for Wilt and the Jayhawks, however, and Kansas delighted the heavily biased Kansas crowd by cruising to an 80–56 victory.

The title game was a dream matchup for fans: top-ranked North Carolina versus second-ranked Kansas. The North Carolina Tarheels had a spotless 31–0 record on the season, but still, Kansas was favored to win the game, largely because they were playing so close to home.

North Carolina came out on fire, building an early 19–7 lead. The Tarheels defense focused on Wilt, and the rest of the Kansas players were missing open shots. Kansas wasn't about to go away, however. Late in the first half and early in the second half, they made a run, eventually taking the lead. With ten minutes to play and a 40–37 lead, Kansas began the same stalling technique that SMU had used on them a few games earlier— with much the same results. North Carolina tied the game late. At 46–46, the game was headed into overtime—only the second overtime in the history of the title game.

The teams appeared tight in the overtime session. On offense, both teams stalled, and each made just one basket in the five-minute period. With nothing settled, the game moved on to a second overtime. If the first overtime had seemed slow and careful, the second was even worse. In five minutes, neither team scored a single basket. Wilt never even got to try a shot.

Finally, in the third overtime, the action picked up. North Carolina came out shooting and built a quick 52–48 lead. Then Wilt got the ball down low and made a basket as a North Carolina defender fouled him. When Wilt drained his free throw, the score was 52–51. On the next possession, Kansas's Maurice King made a free throw to tie the score once again.

Yet another Kansas free throw gave the Jayhawks a 53–52 lead and sent the crowd into a frenzy. Only ten seconds remained in the game. All Kansas had to do was play good defense and the title was theirs.

North Carolina hurried the ball down the court. Tarheel Joe Quigg drove the ball toward the basket, right at Wilt, who was ready to swat away any shot. But Quigg never got to shoot. King went for a steal and fouled Quigg in the process. With five seconds left on the clock, Quigg had two free-throw attempts. After a time-out, Quigg calmly drained both free throws to give North Carolina a 54–53 lead. Kansas had one last desperate chance. They inbounded the ball and then lobbed a high pass toward Wilt at the basket. But the long lob pass was off target, and the Tarheels deflected it away. The game was over.

The Tarheels celebrated a championship and a perfect season, while the Jayhawks looked on, stunned and disappointed. Later, people would call the game the greatest NCAA title game in history, but that was little consolation to Wilt and his teammates. Wilt would later describe the loss as the most bitter of his entire career.

"I've never seen a locker room in my life where people were so devastated," wrote a Lawrence, Kansas, reporter about the mood of the team after the loss.

Wilt was named the Most Valuable Player (MVP) of the 1957 NCAA Tournament. It was only the second time in history the honor had gone to a member of a team that did not win the championship.

After the season, Wilt was named to the All-American team as one of the nation's best college players. Again, he competed with the track team, winning the Big Seven high jump with a mark of 6 feet 5 inches. However, rumors swirled that he would leave the university to pursue a professional basketball career. Wilt was enjoying his college years, though, and he decided instead to return for the 1957–1958 season in hopes of winning the national title that had eluded him the season before.

GETTING AWAY

Wilt spent much of his time in Lawrence with local business owner Roy Edwards and his wife, Joan, largely to escape the attention he got on campus. He'd also play basketball with neighborhood children.

"[Wilt] was like a magnet," Joan Edwards later recalled. "He would lift those little kids so they could put the ball in the basket. And he used to kid even me. He'd say, 'You want a boost?'"

Wilt was socially active at Kansas. A friend would later remember that Wilt was determined to find a young woman to marry. He wanted someone who loved him, not for his fame but for who he was. He dated frequently and met lots of young women but could not find one to settle on.

Wilt's junior season came with mixed results. On the positive side, Wilt set a school record by averaging 30.1 points per game and was again named an All-American. But he also missed some time due to illness. The team finished 18–5, good for just second place in the conference.

That meant Kansas would not be returning to the NCAA Tournament.

An Unwanted Legacy

Kansas paid a steep price for the three years Wilt played there. After he left the school, the NCAA investigated Kansas for violating policies regarding paying players. Although individual names were not released, it was widely believed that people close to the university had given money and gifts to Wilt. This was against the rules.

In 1960 the NCAA handed down a punishment to the university. Kansas could not participate in the NCAA Tournament for two years.

Wilt did not look forward to the prospect of another season of college basketball. He decided that it was time for him to earn a paycheck. He made his announcement in an article he wrote for *Look* magazine. (The magazine paid him $10,000 for the exclusive rights to the announcement.) In the article, he said the college game was not fun since opposing teams used such extreme tactics against him. He further explained that he wanted to help his family's financial situation. He wanted to allow his parents to retire and live comfortably.

There was one problem. An NBA rule said that a player could not join an NBA team until his high school class had graduated from college. For Wilt, that meant that he couldn't join the NBA until 1959—another year. But that didn't stop Wilt from earning a paycheck. He'd found another option.

Chapter | Three

Going Pro

In 1958 the NBA wasn't the only way for a talented young basketball player to earn a living. In fact, the most famous basketball team in the nation wasn't even a part of the NBA. The Harlem Globetrotters was an all-black team that had started as a member of a small league. The Globetrotters had grown into something different, however. They had become a high-flying exhibition team, filled with uniquely talented players. While a big part of the Globetrotters' appeal was in the comic routine they performed on the basketball court, the team was also highly competitive. As recently as 1948, the Globetrotters had defeated the NBA champion Minneapolis Lakers in an exhibition game.

In 1958 Wilt signed a contract to join the Globetrotters. The contract paid him an enormous sum of $65,000—a figure that dwarfed most NBA salaries. Included in that salary was a

$10,000 signing bonus. Wilt took that money and bought a new house for his family and a car for his dad.

The Globetrotters lived up to their name. They played exhibition games all around the globe. Wilt joined the team in Italy while it was on a fifteen-nation tour, playing against a team of college all-stars. Normally, the 7-foot-1 Wilt would be a center. But the Globetrotters were more interested in novelty and show than in winning basketball games, so they played him at the guard position (normally reserved for shorter, more agile players). He learned the team's many comedy routines and fit in seamlessly. His role forced him to concentrate on his dribbling, passing, and ball-handling skills. But the routines also gave him plenty of time to show off rim-rattling dunks.

Wilt would later describe his time with the Globetrotters as the most fun he ever had playing basketball. The team was all about showing off and having fun. There was no pressure to constantly win. The team's only goal was to please the fans. These games were a chance for fans to see him in a new light.

No matter how much Wilt liked being a Harlem Globetrotter, he understood that his future lay in the NBA. There, he could measure himself against the game's best. So in May 1959, he signed a contract with the Philadelphia Warriors. For his rookie season, Wilt would be paid $30,000. The sum seemed small compared to his contract with the Globetrotters. But by NBA standards, the fee was extraordinary. Wilt hadn't played a single minute in the NBA, and already he was the league's highest-paid player.

Could Wilt possibly live up to such a big contract? After all, he would no longer be dominating college athletes. He would be playing against the best basketball players in the world. And traditionally, NBA rookies weren't star players. Usually, a year or two of playing pro ball was needed before a player started to realize his full potential.

But some players knew that Wilt's size would make him a force in the NBA right from the start. "A small man like me doesn't have much chance with Wilt," said 6-foot-9 Clyde Lovellette of the St. Louis Hawks. "He's the toughest offensive pivot man in the league right now and he hasn't played his first official game."

Wilt's NBA debut came on October 24, 1959, in New York. The Warriors were playing the Knicks in the famous Madison Square Garden arena. If there were any doubts about whether Wilt was worth his big contract, he erased them that night. He dominated on both ends of the court, scoring 43 points, grabbing 28 rebounds, and blocking shot after shot on defense. (The NBA didn't count blocked shots as an official statistic until 1973.) The Warriors won the game, 118–109.

How Big Was He?

Wilt's exact height was a matter of question. Some sources list him as 7 feet tall. Others say he was 7 feet 1, and still others list him at 7 feet 2. Some teammates, meanwhile, swore that he stood a full 7 feet 3. Regardless, the NBA listed his official height at a fraction over 7 feet 1 inch.

A week later, Wilt and the Warriors played their first home game, against the Detroit Pistons. Philadelphia was where Wilt would truly earn his paycheck. Excitement about the team and its new hometown star was high.

A record crowd of 9,112 turned out to see Wilt's first NBA game in Philadelphia. And once again, he did not disappoint. In a 120–112 Warrior victory, he netted 36 points and grabbed 34 rebounds.

The team moved to 3–0 on the young season before Wilt faced his first big challenge. The Warriors traveled to Boston to take on the Celtics. Boston, led by center Bill Russell, was the league's best team. Prior to Wilt's entry to the NBA, Russell was the biggest name in the sport. The Russell-Chamberlain matchup was the best the NBA had to offer and was the beginning of one of the greatest rivalries in NBA history.

"I don't plan to do anything particular about Russell or anyone else," Wilt said. "I'm just doing everything I can to be ready for everybody. I'm playing them all alike. And they all better be mean."

According to Wilt, early in his professional career, he had a vertical jump of 50 inches. That's six inches higher than the great basketball star Michael Jordan could jump. Wilt, however, earned a reputation for exaggerating his own abilities.

Wilt quickly discovered that Russell was a worthy opponent. Wilt could not score at will, as he had in his three previous NBA contests. Russell stood a few inches shorter than Wilt, but his athleticism, experience, and tenacity made him a match for Wilt. And Russell had the benefit of being surrounded by talent. The Celtics did not rely on him for everything, which wasn't the case with the Warriors and Wilt. Wilt did score a game-high 30 points, but he needed to take 38 shots to get there. Meanwhile, Russell netted 20 points. The Celtics were clearly the superior team and handed the Warriors their first loss of the season, 115–106.

By November 25, Philly's record was 9–5 and Wilt was leading the NBA both in scoring and rebounding. Next up was a home-and-away series that had everyone excited. The Celtics hosted the Warriors again on November 25, and the two teams traveled to Philadelphia the next day for a Thanksgiving tilt. Back-to-back Russell-Chamberlain games were an NBA fan's dream.

This time around, Wilt and the Warriors were prepared. Wilt left no debate as to which player was the best on the floor. He dominated at both ends, scoring 45 points and securing 35 rebounds while holding Russell to 15 points and 13 rebounds.

Philly cruised to a 123–113 victory, and Wilt proved that even though his NBA career was just a month old, there wasn't anybody in the league who could stop him when he was at his best. And if the first victory wasn't enough, the Warriors won again on Thanksgiving, this time giving the Philly fans cause to celebrate with a 143–130 win.

In 1959 Wilt bought a harness-racing horse. His horse, named Spooky Cadet, was the first of several he owned. Horse racing—and betting on horse races—would be a hobby Wilt would enjoy for most of his life.

As the season went on, Philly kept winning and Wilt kept lighting up the scoreboard. Soon NBA opponents felt like Wilt's college opponents had felt. They resorted to beating and banging on Wilt, treating him roughly and hoping he missed enough free throws to keep them in the game.

"Everybody says to knock the other guy off the court," Wilt said of the physical treatment. "That's not my way. I just want to play my normal game. But if it keeps going like this, I guess I'll have to punch somebody in the mouth."

The rough treatment continued. In one game, Lovellette bashed his elbow into Wilt's mouth, loosening two front teeth (which later had to be pulled) and severely cutting the inside of Wilt's lip. Wilt's mouth hurt so badly that he couldn't even eat. But a liquid diet didn't stop him from going out the next night and scoring 41 points and, in the process, breaking the NBA record for total points in a season. Wilt broke the record in his 56th game, with still 19 more games to play!

Wilt's rookie season wasn't just good. It was completely ridiculous. He averaged 37.6 points and 27 rebounds per game. He blocked shots at an unheard-of pace. No rookie in any major pro sport had ever dominated a league so thoroughly. Wilt's only weakness was his free-throw shooting. He made only 58 percent of his foul shots. Predictably, he was named the league's Rookie of the Year and MVP for his efforts.

The year before Wilt joined the team, Philadelphia's record had been 32–40. With Wilt, they finished 49–26, good enough for second place in the NBA's Eastern Division and a spot in the playoffs. At the time, three teams in each division made the playoffs. The Eastern Division winner (the Celtics) played the winner of a series between the second- and third-place teams. The Warriors defeated the third-place Syracuse Nationals two games to one to set up yet another matchup with the Celtics.

Wilt was named to the Eastern Division All-Star team in his rookie year. He scored 23 points and collected 25 rebounds en route to being named the All-Star Game MVP.

The Eastern Division Finals was a best-of-seven series— the first team to win four advanced to the NBA Finals. Wilt understood that the playoffs were where winning truly mattered, and no team was more playoff-tested than Boston. The Celtics proved why they were the favorites to win by taking Game 1, 111–105.

Philadelphia bounced back in the second game, winning 115–110 to tie the series. But the win came with a steep cost. The Celtics, as expected, played a very rough and physical style of basketball against Wilt. At one point, Wilt became fed up with the treatment. He shoved Boston's Tom Heinsohn, who promptly shoved him back. During the altercation, Wilt somehow hurt his hand, and the injury slowed him for the next several games. He was clearly in pain during a Game 3 loss, in which he scored just 12 points. Boston took advantage and won the next two games to take a 3–1 series lead.

During Wilt's rookie season in the NBA, he'd considered quitting basketball to pursue his love for track and field. He wanted to compete in track's ultimate event, the decathlon, in which athletes perform in ten different track-and-field events. "I'm convinced I can break the world decathlon record, and I want to give it a try," he said.

The Warriors were in a deep hole. They had to win the next three games to advance to the finals. They did manage to win Game 5 behind Wilt's 50-point performance, but the Celtics closed out the series in Game 6, ending a remarkable season for the big rookie.

Wilt was fed up. He'd hoped the NBA would be different, but the rough treatment he got in the pros was little different from what he'd suffered at the college level. Wilt had other ideas. The frustration of losing to Boston pushed Wilt over the edge. He shocked Philly fans and basketball fans worldwide with an announcement. "I quit," he said on March 25, 1960. "I'll never play basketball in the NBA again."

Chapter Four

Back in Action

Wilt's announcement that he was quitting the NBA got quite a reaction. Fans and media called him a quitter. They said that things had come so easily to Wilt all his life that he didn't know how to deal with adversity. Others said that they flatly didn't believe him. Warriors owner Eddie Gottlieb said that until Wilt didn't show up for the 1960–1961 season, he didn't believe that Wilt was really done.

Wilt showed that he was serious, however. He traveled to Chicago to rejoin the Globetrotters and then took off with the team for a tour of Europe. But somewhere along the way, Wilt had a change of heart. Gottlieb talked him into returning to the Warriors, signing him to a three-year contract. The first year of the contract would pay Wilt $65,000. The amounts for the following years were left blank. Wilt trusted that Gottlieb would pay him what he was worth to the team.

The 1960–1961 season was filled with highs and lows for Wilt. Once again, he was the most dominant individual player in the league. In what many consider the most impressive performance of his NBA career, he collected an NBA-record 55 rebounds in a November 24 game against the Celtics. But even that wasn't enough, as the Warriors lost the game 132–129.

Fans and media were starting to question whether Wilt was really a winner. After all, he'd failed to win a national title at Kansas, and the Warriors still looked as if they were a long way away from competing with the Celtics. Russell said that such criticism was nonsense. "I can't understand how some people get off criticizing Wilt," he said. "What more can they ask him to do?"

66*Why does everyone want to ridicule [Wilt]? . . . It isn't Wilt versus Russell, but Wilt versus the world.*99

—FRANK McGUIRE, DEFENDING WILT
AFTER A GAME IN BOSTON

For the season, Wilt broke his own scoring record, averaging 38.4 points per game. He also averaged 27.2 rebounds. He became the first player in league history to score 3,000 points in a season and also the first (and to date the only) to grab 2,000 rebounds.

The Warriors again finished in second place to Boston, with a record of 46–33. As they had in the previous year, they played Syracuse in the first round of the playoffs. This time it was a best-of-five series. But fans looking forward to another Russell-Chamberlain matchup would be disappointed. Wilt—and the rest of the Philly team, for that matter—struggled badly at the free-throw stripe. Syracuse swept the Warriors.

In 1961 Wilt helped buy a jazz club in Harlem (a New York City neighborhood) called Big Wilt's Small's Paradise.

Wilt was unhappy during his second season, and he wasn't afraid to let others know about it. He sulked about officiating. He yelled at coach Neil Johnston. He got mad at teammates and refused to talk to anyone for days at a time. "He was in a world of his own," said one of his fellow players.

Gottlieb knew his team needed a change. People said that Wilt and Johnston didn't always see eye-to-eye. So Gottlieb fired Johnston and replaced him with Frank McGuire. McGuire was no stranger to Wilt. He had coached the North Carolina team that had defeated Wilt's Kansas team in the 1957 NCAA title game. McGuire was a strong-willed coach with a proven track record. Still, Wilt admitted that he wasn't sure he wanted to play for the man who had dealt him the most painful loss of his career.

McGuire spoke to the troubled player soon after his signing. "That first meeting, I told Wilt that I realized he was a famous player with a national reputation to consider. Then I said I had a national reputation to consider, too. Wilt said he was willing to try anything I thought would help the team. With that attitude and all his talent I found myself wondering if the uncoachable Chamberlain might not be a coach's dream."

Chamberlain proved to be exactly that in the 1961–1962 season. After another summer spent with the Globetrotters, he returned to Philly to begin what would be perhaps the greatest season any individual NBA player has ever enjoyed. Despite some early struggles, the Warriors put together another decent season. Wilt scored at rates almost beyond imagination.

On December 8, 1961, the Warriors lost a triple-overtime game to the Los Angeles Lakers. Wilt broke the single-game scoring record by netting 78 points in the losing effort. In January he scored 73 points in a 135–117 victory over Chicago, setting the mark for a non-overtime game. His level of scoring was so outrageous that people started to criticize him for it.

"[Wilt is] nothing but a scoring machine," said Chicago Packers coach Jim Pollard. "The idea of the game isn't to score points. The idea is to win."

Others spoke out against the officiating. "Nobody can breathe on [Wilt] without getting a foul called," said Syracuse coach Alex Hannum.

For some reason, Wilt's performance only seemed to bring on more criticism. People accused him of making a mockery of the league. Even the Philadelphia fans seemed to be bored with their star, and attendance for the club began to dip. Sensational media stories said that Wilt yelled at fellow Warriors players if they took a shot instead of passing him the ball.

According to McGuire, Wilt, and the rest of the Philly players, however, there was absolutely no truth to those accusations. Still, the damage was done. Wilt's success was somehow making him less and less popular. He was becoming a player that many fans loved to hate.

The season was epitomized in Wilt's famous 100-point game March 2, 1962. By season's end, Wilt had a bushel of new records. His scoring average of 50.4 points per game was off the charts. He became the first and only NBA player ever to score

4,000 points in a season. He added 25.7 rebounds per game. And while some accused him of shooting too often, he made almost 51 percent of the shots he took, a very good percentage in the NBA.

Wilt's 100-point game was not televised. The only recording that exists is a partial radio broadcast. A fan had recorded part of the game at home. Without that fan's recording, we would have nothing but the official box score and the recollections of those present to mark the amazing performance.

Wilt's efforts weren't enough for the Warriors to overtake the Celtics in the standings, however. For the third straight year, they finished in second place, with a 49–31 record. And once again, Philadelphia faced Syracuse in the first round of the playoffs. This time, Wilt and the Warriors exacted revenge, beating the Nationals in a deciding Game 5, 121–104, for the right to do battle with Russell and the Celtics.

The Eastern Division Finals was a fantastic series. As a result of having finished in first place, Boston held the home court advantage, meaning they would have four home games to Philly's three. That proved to be important.

"We took them to the limit," Wilt later said of the series. "They were a great basketball team. We were becoming a great basketball team."

But to everyone's surprise, if the Warriors were to become a great team, it would not be in Philadelphia. Change was in the air.

Chapter | Five

Westward Bound

Only a month after Warriors fans had been disappointed by their team's loss in the Eastern Division Finals, they got even worse news. A group of business owners had made Gottlieb an offer he couldn't refuse—$850,000 for the team. The new ownership announced that the team would move to San Francisco for the 1962–1963 season. The Warriors and their hometown hero were leaving Philadelphia.

For Wilt, San Francisco was a new, exciting place. The weather was nicer than in Philly, and there was a whole new group of women for him to date. Wilt had long before stopped trying to find a wife. Instead, he seemed determined to date as many women as was humanly possible. Some close to him thought he was making up for his younger years, when girls had rejected him. Whatever his reasons, Wilt was happy with the move, which felt like a fresh start.

San Francisco fans never really accepted Wilt as their own, however, and the problem was not unique to Wilt. Baseball's New York Giants had moved to San Francisco a few years before, and the city's baseball fans were extremely slow to embrace future Hall of Famer Willie Mays as well. Like Mays had before him, Wilt faced resistance when he tried to buy a house in an all-white neighborhood. In both cases, the sale eventually went through. But for the two men, their introduction to a new city had been less than welcome.

McGuire resigned and didn't make the trip west with the team. So the Warriors hired former NBA player and California native Bob Feerick to be the team's third coach in three years. And the team itself was somewhat dismantled. Paul Arizin refused to move with the team and retired. Tom Gola requested a trade early in the season and was sent back east. Wilt had less experienced help than ever.

The results were predictable. More than ever, opposing teams zeroed in on Wilt. Wilt did his part, averaging 44.8 points and 24.3 rebounds per game, but the rest of the team played miserably. Their final record of 31–49 was the second worst in the NBA.

The 1963–1964 season saw even more change. Yet another new ownership group took over the team, and they brought in the team's fourth coach in four years. Former Syracuse coach

Alex Hannum was a proven winner, and he was familiar with Wilt's skills and temperament. In addition, Hannum was a former sergeant in the U.S. Army. His players called him Sarge, and they understood that it was his way or the highway. The change was a good fit for Wilt, who needed a strong-willed coach to command his respect.

One sportswriter predicted the change would make no difference. "Chamberlain is a loser. Has been all his life. Neither his college nor his pro team has ever won a title, because he won't take coaching. All he wants to do is score points."

But that sportswriter was wrong. The difference in Wilt was like night and day. Hannum told Wilt to pass the ball more, and Wilt listened. In the past, when Wilt got the ball down low, everybody in the arena knew he was going to shoot it. The defenders who weren't guarding him at the time could relax and just watch and wait for a rebound. But this season, things were different. Wilt didn't take every shot he could get. He kicked the ball back out to wide-open teammates. That created a new set of problems for defenses.

The Warriors won five of their first seven games, setting a winning tone for the new season. The Western Division was still weaker than the East, especially because the normally powerful Lakers were missing two of their best players due to injury, and the Warriors took advantage of that.

"How could such a bad team suddenly become so good?" asked *Sports Illustrated* writer Tom Brody. "There are two reasons. The first, of course, is Chamberlain, a player Ed Macauley [a Celtic] once called the worst in the world because he wasn't doing what he could do. Now he is one of the best because he is doing just that. The other reason is Alex Hannum."

❝*I am tired of being a villain. It is not the role I had in mind when I entered this sport. I don't feel like a villain, and I don't think like a villain.*❞
—WILT ON HIS ROLE AS A PLAYER MANY FANS LOVED TO HATE

With basically the same team that had struggled so badly a season before, the Warriors finished in first place in the Western Division. Wilt's scoring average dropped to 36.9 points per game, but he averaged 5 assists per game—by far his career high to that date. In the Western Division Finals, the Warriors squared off with the St. Louis Hawks. St. Louis played them hard, but the new and improved Wilt proved too much to handle. San Francisco advanced with a 4–3 series win.

For the first time in his career, Wilt was headed to the NBA Finals. There, he and the Warriors would face a familiar foe in the Celtics. Boston took care of business at home in Game 1, holding Wilt to 22 points and claiming a 108–96 victory.

The best thing that ever happened to the NBA is that God made Wilt a nice man. He could have killed us all with that left hand.

— JACK MCMAHON, FORMER NBA PLAYER AND COACH

That set up what was, for all the wrong reasons, a memorable Game 2. Boston's Clyde Lovellette was in the game, shoving Wilt all over the court. Lovellette was known as something of a dirty player. He was also the man who had knocked two of Wilt's teeth loose with a vicious elbow a few years before. On this night, Wilt had had enough of Lovellette's bullying style. Referee Norm Drucker later recalled the exchange that came as a result: "Wilt said [to Lovellette] 'Cut it out,' or words to that effect. With that, Clyde put his hands up in a fighting pose. I think Wilt thought Clyde was going to throw a punch, so Wilt hit him right in the jaw. Clyde crumpled to the floor."

Warriors forward Tom Meschery added, "I can tell you, the punch didn't travel more than 10 inches. Clyde fell like a bull in a bullfight."

Players and coaches from both teams stormed out, and the court turned into bedlam. The police had to come out to restore order. Wilt took a lot of punishment and almost never fought back, but when he did, he made his point. Lovellette would think twice about bullying the Big Dipper again. While Wilt may have won the battle, the Celtics won the war, extending their series lead to 2–0 with a 124–121 victory.

The series moved to San Francisco for Game 3. Back at home, the Warriors built a huge early lead and cruised to a 115–91 victory. It was their only win of the series, however. Boston won the next two games to claim yet another NBA title.

Once again, Wilt had to live with the "loser" label that had been heaped upon him, and once again he seriously thought about retiring from the NBA. This time, he considered pursuing a pro football career. He even worked out at a clinic for the Kansas City Chiefs, catching passes.

The notion of switching sports soon passed, however. Wilt was back in San Francisco to begin the 1964–1965 season. After their trip to the NBA Finals, fans had high hopes for the Warriors that season. But not all was well. Wilt wasn't feeling well in the fall of 1964. He had chest pains. Doctors didn't know what was wrong with him. At first, they believed that he'd had a small heart attack. But later, they determined that the problem was pancreatitis, an inflammation or infection of the pancreas.

Wilt missed the beginning of the season as he battled the problem. He lost a lot of weight. Some reports said he dropped 50 pounds, though his doctor later said it was more like 15. When Wilt finally returned to the Warriors, he was out of shape. Predictably, the Warriors struggled.

THE WARRIORS

The Warriors franchise was founded in Philadelphia in 1946 as an original member of the Basketball Association of America (which became the NBA in 1949). The Philadelphia Warriors won the league's first championship, in 1947.

The team moved to San Francisco in 1962, but the city never fully embraced the Warriors. By the late 1960s, the Warriors were playing many of their games in nearby Oakland. They moved full-time to Oakland in 1971.

With the move, they changed their name to the Golden State Warriors. The team's name remains the only one in the NBA that does not include a city or state name, though the Golden State is a nickname for California.

Wilt's health was only the beginning of the problems for the Warriors. As a business, the franchise was doing terribly. The team had lost money even during its successful 1963–1964 campaign. As the team kept losing, attendance dropped and the owners were losing more money than ever.

A big part of the problem was Wilt's salary. He made more money than the rest of the players on the team combined. The Warriors had to do something, and the decision they made shocked the basketball world. In January 1965, the Warriors traded Wilt to the Philadelphia 76ers for three players and cash. (The 76ers had formerly been the Syracuse Nationals. They had moved to Philadelphia after the Warriors moved to San Francisco.)

Wilt was leaving the only NBA organization he'd ever been with. But he was also going home.

Chapter Six

Home to Philly

Acquiring Wilt was a big deal for the 76ers. The Philly fans had been slow to warm to their new team. After all, for years the Syracuse Nationals had been one of the Warriors' biggest rivals. Bringing Wilt to the team gave the 76ers more of a hometown flavor.

The Philly fans knew Wilt, and many had still rooted for him in San Francisco. And of course, adding the best player in the league couldn't hurt either. In fact, it was the first time in NBA history that the league's scoring leader had been traded during a season.

Wilt had mixed feelings about the move. "Going back home was nice, but I had fallen in love with San Francisco, and I was rather sad to leave," he said.

Any second thoughts Wilt might have had were erased in his first game with his new team. The Philly fans packed the arena and gave him a thunderous ovation. They cheered and kept cheering for fifteen minutes. Wilt was so touched that he shed a few tears on the court. He later said the warm homecoming was "the greatest thing that has ever happened to me in sports."

The 76ers ended the season at 40–40, third in the East. Between his two teams that season, Wilt played in 73 games, averaging 34.7 points and 22.9 rebounds per game.

Even with Wilt, the 76ers were underdogs in their opening playoff series against the Cincinnati Royals. But Philadelphia won the opening game in overtime and never looked back, winning the series 3–1. The win sent the team to the Eastern Division Finals. Once again, Russell and the powerful Celtics stood in the way of Wilt's NBA title dreams.

"This has been a long, long year for me," Wilt wrote in an article for *Sports Illustrated*. "Here I am again, in the finals for the Eastern Division NBA title. Once again, facing my old friend Bill Russell of the Boston Celtics. If we win this one, fine. If we lose this one I know already what a lot of people are going to say, because I've heard it all before, you know? A lot of people will say . . . old Wilt is a loser."

It was another great series. The teams split the first four games, with the home team winning every time. Boston took a 3–2 series lead in Game 5, meaning that the 76ers had to win the final two games to advance to the NBA Finals.

Wilt and his teammates came through in Game 6. It was a dicey affair, though. Wilt racked up five fouls and played the end of the game knowing that another foul would mean the end of his night. The Celtics went after him on play after play, trying to draw that sixth foul. But Wilt continued to play aggressive defense, all the while avoiding a foul. His presence on both offense and defense gave the 76ers the victory (112–106) they needed to stay alive.

❝Wilt and [Bill] Russell was the first great matchup in the league. Those two and their head-to-head battles are the reason the league got to be so popular.❞

—BILL SHARMAN, WILT'S COACH AND
RUSSELL'S FORMER TEAMMATE

The deciding Game 7 would be played in Boston. Wilt was fantastic in the game, making 12 of his 15 shots from the field, scoring 30 points, and collecting 32 rebounds. He also held Russell to just 16 points on the night.

Wilt was at his best in the game's final minute, as he and the 76ers tried to erase a small Celtics lead. He made two free throws with 36 seconds left. With less than 10 seconds to go, the Boston lead was three points. Wilt got the ball low and threw down a powerful dunk over Russell to cut the margin to one point. Boston turned over the ball on the following possession. The 76ers had the ball, trailing 110–109, with just five seconds left in the game.

Philly coach Dolph Schayes decided not to throw the ball directly to Wilt, fearing that Boston would immediately foul him to send him to the free-throw line. Even though Wilt had just made two free throws, he was just 6 of 13 in the game and Schayes didn't want the outcome to come down to the weakest part of Wilt's game. Instead, the 76ers planned to throw the ball in to a guard, who would take a quick shot. The idea was that if the shot missed, Wilt would be there to collect a rebound and score an easy basket. But Boston stole the inbounds pass, securing the 110–109 victory. The season was over for the 76ers, and Wilt had never even gotten to touch the ball on his team's final possession.

The ABC television network hired Wilt to work as a broadcaster for the 1965 NBA Finals. Wilt's job was to be the "color commentator." In this role, he explained the inner workings of the game to the television audience.

Wilt participates in the shot put event for Overbrook High School in 1955.

Wilt *(bottom, center)* was part of the Boys' Athletic Association during his senior year at Overbrook High School in Philadelphia, Pennsylvania.

Wilt grabs a rebound for Kansas during a 1956 game against Iowa State.

Wilt played for the Harlem Globetrotters in 1959.

Wilt celebrates his 100-point game in the locker room on March 2, 1962.

Wilt *(right)* and Celtics center Bill Russell had a storied rivalry throughout their careers. This photo is from a 1966 playoff game when Wilt was playing for the Philadelphia 76ers.

AP Photo

Wilt is presented with a backboard and hoop trophy in 1972 after he became the NBA's all-time leading rebounder.

In 1984, Wilt appeared in *Conan the Destroyer* as Bombaata.

Wilt shows two kids how to hit a volleyball at a sports clinic in 1985. Wilt played volleyball throughout his life.

Wilt speaks at a news conference in 1998 for the retirement of his jersey number at the University of Kansas.

Wilt still talked about retirement (this time he wanted to become a professional boxer!), but the talk again faded and he returned for the 1965–1966 NBA season. The 76ers signed Wilt to a new three-year contract worth $100,000 per year.

Philly entered the new season with high hopes. They'd taken Boston to the brink in the Eastern Division Finals, and now they'd have Wilt for the full season. The enthusiasm was well placed.

The 76ers of 1965–1966 were probably the most talented team Wilt had played for in his NBA career to date, and they lived up to expectations. They battled for the Eastern Division lead all season. A season-ending eleven-game winning streak propelled them to the division crown. The team clinched the division in the last game of the season.

With his average of 33.5 points, 24.6 rebounds, and 5.2 assists per game, Wilt earned his second league MVP award after the season. He also eclipsed the league's all-time record for points, formerly held by Bob Pettit. Wilt wasn't scoring as much as he had in his younger days, but he remained the game's most dominant player, and finally he was on a first-place team.

As division winners, the 76ers didn't have to play in the first round of the playoffs. Boston and Cincinnati squared off for the right to play Philly in the division finals. Predictably, the Celtics prevailed. As well as the regular season had gone for Philly, the end result was disappointingly familiar. Boston dominated Wilt and the 76ers in the playoffs, winning the series four games to one, and again, Wilt had to watch his biggest rival celebrate.

The Celtics went on to win the 1966 NBA title. It was their eighth straight championship, a feat unmatched in major team sports.

Wilt was again wide open to criticism. The "loser" label that had followed him for so many years wasn't going to go away until Wilt earned an NBA title. Some claimed that Wilt was not giving his full commitment to the 76ers. Wilt chose to live in New York and commute to Philadelphia. He liked to sleep in, and because Schayes wanted to accommodate his star, the 76ers scheduled late afternoon practices rather than the customary morning practices.

Worst of all, Wilt had flatly refused to attend a team practice after Game 3 of the playoff series with Boston and then showed up late before Game 5. Some of the criticism Wilt received was undeserved, but his sometimes unprofessional behavior gave his critics more than ample cause to rip on him. Worse still, he was giving teammates reason to question his commitment.

"There are some people—I won't call them fans, because they don't know the first thing about the game—who shout that I'm selfish if I take 30 shots. It's nothing new. I've been hearing it for years. If I scored 40, I shot too much. If I scored 20, I was dogging it [not playing hard enough]."

—WILT CHAMBERLAIN, 1966

Schayes clearly had lost control of his star player and his team. So not surprisingly, the 76ers fired him after the season. The team needed a coach who would command Wilt's respect. With Alex Hannum available, the choice was easy. If anybody could get Wilt in line, it was his former coach. Even though Wilt and Hannum were often at odds, Hannum always stood his ground. Wilt and the rest of the team knew exactly who was in charge. Hannum would not tolerate some of the behavior Wilt had displayed the previous season.

"Alex [Hannum] never backed down," said forward Billy Cunningham. "I think the way the coach handled [Wilt] showed us who was going to be the boss."

Would a change at the helm make the difference for the 76ers? The 1966–1967 season would tell the story.

Chapter Seven

A New Wilt

Hannum took over a team loaded with talent. The loss to the Celtics had made many forget what a great regular season Philly had enjoyed. They would be expected to turn in a similar performance during the 1966–1967 season, and Wilt, the league's reigning MVP, would once again have to lead the way. But Hannum stressed that Wilt would have to lead in a different way. The 76ers didn't need him to take so many shots. They needed him to rebound, play great defense, and let the talented players around him play their parts. If he could do that—if he could reinvent himself—there was no telling what the 76ers might achieve.

Early on, the team more than lived up to expectations. They won their first seven games and fifteen of their first sixteen. After a November 23 loss to the Royals, they ripped off an eleven-game winning streak, immediately followed by another eleven-game winning streak. By January 23, they had a ridiculous record of 45–4. Even the Celtics had never dominated the league so thoroughly. The 76ers had a 9.5-game lead over the second-place Celtics and cruised to a second straight Eastern Division title with a 68–13 record—the greatest regular season in terms of winning percentage in NBA history.

Ironically, Wilt averaged a career-low 24.1 points per game in what was his best regular season from a team standpoint. For the first time, he didn't win the league's scoring title. He passed the ball like never before, averaging 7.8 assists per game, a career high at the time. Even with a scoring average of less than half of what he'd achieved in 1961–1962, Wilt was named league MVP—the third time he'd been so honored.

At one point during the 1966–1967 season, Wilt made 35 straight field goal attempts—an NBA record that still stands.

Even though the 76ers had won the division, they still had to play an opening-round playoff series (beginning that year, four teams from each division made the playoffs). They beat Cincinnati four games to one to advance to the Eastern Division

Finals, where they faced the Celtics. The series promised to be an exciting matchup. Wilt had a solid team around him, while Russell and the defending champs were beginning to show signs of aging. Wilt was fantastic in Game 1, posting 24 points, 32 rebounds, 13 assists, and 12 blocks. The 76ers won the game 127–113 to take control of the series.

They weren't about to let Boston back in the series. Wilt was a defensive power in Game 2, forcing Boston players into bad shots and leading his team to a tight 107–102 victory. "Wilt is proving that he's the greatest player that ever lived," Hannum said after the game. "And that's one reason I want the title so much—to prove that he is."

Wilt and the 76ers kept going. In Game 3, Wilt grabbed a playoff-record 41 rebounds in a 115–104 victory. "I've never moved so much in my life," Wilt said of his activity in Game 3. "Not even the night I scored 100 [points]."

Boston avoided the sweep by winning Game 4, but the 76ers closed them out in Game 5 to earn a trip to the NBA Finals. For the first time in eight seasons, someone other than the Celtics would celebrate an NBA title. Would it be Wilt and the 76ers?

The team that stood in their way was familiar to Wilt and the Philly fans. It was Wilt's old team, the San Francisco Warriors. The series started with a bang in Game 1—a 141–135 overtime victory for Philly. Game 2 wasn't nearly as competitive, with the 76ers thrashing the Warriors 126–95. Wilt struggled with his shooting in the game, especially at the foul line (he made just two of seventeen shots). But his great defense and rebounding more than made up for his struggles, and guard Hal Greer picked up the scoring slack with 30 points.

Like many big men throughout NBA history, Wilt struggled with free-throw shooting for his entire career. In 1966–1967, he tried a new tactic: shooting underhanded. It didn't help, as Wilt made only 44 percent of his foul shots that season.

Just when the 76ers looked like they would run away with the series, San Francisco fought back, winning two of the next three games—helped by Wilt's continual struggle with his shooting. The low point for Philly came at home in Game 5 when they blew a 13-point fourth-quarter lead and lost the game. The 76ers had a 3–2 series lead headed into Game 6 in San Francisco, but the Warriors had momentum on their side. Wilt and the 76ers were eager to close out the series, not wanting to allow the Warriors to force a decisive Game 7.

More than fifteen thousand screaming fans packed the court for the big game. The Warriors rode that support to an early lead, which they carried into the second half. Late in the third quarter, San Francisco seemed firmly in control. The lead grew to 12 points, and the series seemed destined to return to Philly for a final game. After the collapse in Game 5, Philly seemed to be completely falling apart on the court.

But just when things looked their worst, the 76ers fought back. They cut into the San Francisco lead and pulled to within 4 points early in the fourth quarter. Wilt wasn't about to let his team lose the game. He was a quarter away from the one thing in his career that had eluded him, and he wasn't going to let the title slip away. Wilt took over the game, both on the boards and on defense. He grabbed 8 rebounds and blocked 6 shots in the final quarter. His efforts helped the 76ers to take a one-point lead with just fifteen seconds to go.

The Warriors needed a basket to stay alive. Their star, Rick Barry, had the ball. Barry was a scoring machine, so Wilt moved toward him. Barry knew what great defense Wilt had been playing, so he made a quick decision to pass the ball down low to San Francisco center Nate Thurmond. With Wilt out of position, Thurmond would be left with an easy basket. But Wilt anticipated Barry's pass. As Barry picked up his dribble, Wilt quickly shifted back to Thurmond, denying Barry the pass. That left

Barry holding the ball with nobody open and the final seconds ticking away. Barry had no choice but to throw up a bad shot. The shot missed, and Philly took over possession. After two players made free throws, the 76ers had a 125–122 victory and the NBA championship that Wilt had so long coveted.

Wilt was thrilled as he celebrated with his teammates. "It's been a long time coming for me," he said. "And all I can say is that it's wonderful to be a part of the greatest team in basketball."

After the 1966–1967 season, Wilt treated himself to a new car—a Maserati sports car custom built to fit his tall frame. The car could go 170 miles per hour, and if reports about Wilt's fast driving were true, he probably pushed that limit.

All was not well, however. Wilt was embroiled in a dispute with team owner Irv Kosloff. Wilt said that former owner Ike Richman had promised him a 25 percent ownership in the team after his playing career, but no written proof of the agreement existed, and Richman had passed away. Kosloff insisted that he knew nothing of such a deal and that Wilt would not be getting a stake in team ownership. Wilt was livid. He threatened to leave the NBA for the newly formed American Basketball Association (ABA). In the end, Wilt backed off his threat and signed a one-year contract worth $250,000. The amount was the most any player had ever been paid for a season in basketball or in any other team sport.

Wilt went to work that fall to earn his money. He remained a fantastic player, but at the age of thirty-one, he was no longer the dominant force the NBA had known in past years. Still, with a solid team around him, Wilt was finding new ways to beat opponents. In recent years, he had been passing more often. He took this philosophy to a new level in 1967–1968, dishing out a career-high 8.6 assists per game—an unheard-of total for a center. His total of 702 assists led the league. Critics accused Wilt of taking the NBA's assist title merely to spite those who said he didn't pass often enough. Regardless, the pass-first philosophy worked. Once again, the 76ers were among the league's elite teams. They won nine of their first ten games and jumped out to an early lead in the Eastern Division.

Still, Wilt's relative lack of scoring had some people wondering whether he was a shell of his former self. Wilt heard the rumors, and his pride wouldn't allow for the rumors to stick. So in December, he briefly went back to his old style. In two games, he scored 68 and 47 points, respectively, proving that he could still put up huge scoring totals—if he wanted to. That he chose not to was a reflection of a team-first approach that many claimed he had lacked in his younger years. Regardless, Wilt still managed 24.3 points per game, third best in the league. He also collected another league MVP trophy.

TRAGEDY OFF THE COURT

A day before the highly anticipated 1967–1968 Eastern Division Finals, black civil rights leader Dr. Martin Luther King Jr. was shot and killed in Memphis, Tennessee. Many players lobbied the league to postpone the series. King had been a hero to people of all races, including many of the players on both teams.

Even Wilt, who rarely spoke out on social issues, made his thoughts known. "I would personally like to see the whole day taken off as some kind of memorial to Dr. King," he told reporters. "But I'm only one individual. . . . I don't want to instigate anything. I'll follow the majority."

The game went on as planned, though the series' second game was postponed several days to honor a national day of mourning on April 7. Wilt later attended King's funeral.

Philly cruised to first place in the Eastern Division, finishing eight games ahead of second-place Boston. The 76ers opened with a hard-fought series victory over the Knicks. But the victory came at a high price. Star forward Billy Cunningham broke his hand during the series and was out for the rest of the season.

Cunningham's absence would be felt in the next series, against the Celtics. Coming off a title and another brilliant regular season, the 76ers were favored in the series. But the aging Celtics had a few tricks left in their bag. Boston came out hot, stealing the first game on Philadelphia's home court.

The 76ers responded quickly. They won the next three games to take a commanding 3–1 series lead. Wilt was wearing down, battling multiple nagging injuries, though the same was true for Russell. And because the 76ers were the stronger overall team, there seemed little doubt that they'd close out the Celtics and go on as huge favorites in the NBA Finals.

Things didn't work that way, however. Boston won Games 5 and 6 to tie the series. Game 7 would decide the series. If the Celtics could find a way to win one more time, they'd become the first team in NBA history to come back from a 3–1 playoff series deficit. Philly came out looking nervous. They couldn't make their shots and quickly fell behind by 12 points. Boston managed to hold that lead, stunning the Philadelphia crowd with a 100–96 victory. The 76ers' season was over. Shockingly, Wilt took only two shots in the entire second half. With everything on the line, the best player in the league had all but disappeared when it mattered the most. Some blamed Wilt. Others said Philly's coaches failed to get him the ball. Either way, Wilt had not been able to score when his team desperately needed points.

Chapter Eight

The Laker Years

The 76ers' playoff collapse left the franchise in turmoil. Coach Hannum announced that he wouldn't be back for the 1968–1969 season. Hannum even suggested that Wilt replace him as the 76ers coach (although with Wilt's hostility toward ownership, that seemed an unrealistic proposal). Furthermore, Wilt did not have a contract with the team for the upcoming season, and to nobody's surprise, he demanded an ownership stake in the team if he was to return.

That summer Wilt traveled to Los Angeles to be with his parents, who had moved there. His father was ill, and Wilt wanted to be nearby. He said that he wanted to live in Los Angeles. He liked the idea of living in a town filled with stars and celebrities. At over 7 feet tall, he'd never blend in, but at least in Los Angeles, he would stand out a little less. Some suggested that Wilt liked the city for its large pool of attractive young women. Wilt reportedly demanded a trade. If the 76ers refused, he threatened to join the Los Angeles ABA franchise, the Stars.

POLITICAL WILT

Late in his career, Wilt started becoming more outspoken on social and political issues. In 1968 he campaigned for presidential candidate Richard Nixon. He also served as a campaign adviser for Nixon, giving the candidate advice on matters that concerned the African American community. Wilt also spoke out on issues such as racial equality, pointing out that more minorities needed to be hired in positions of power in sports.

The 76ers had little choice. On July 9, 1968, they traded Wilt to the Lakers for three players. Lakers owner Jack Kent Cooke, thrilled at having acquired the league's reigning MVP, rewarded Wilt with a $250,000 contract.

Wilt joined a team stacked with talent. Future Hall of Famers Jerry West and Elgin Baylor had already made the Lakers a force in the league. Adding Wilt to the mix made the Lakers look like a bona fide superpower in the NBA. West and Baylor had known a fate familiar to Wilt—enjoying great success but being unable to get past the dominant Celtics in the NBA Finals. The combined forces of Wilt, West, and Baylor promised, at least in talent, to be the beginning of a new dynasty in the league. Before the season even got under way, the expectations for the team were as high as they could be. Anything short of an NBA title would seem like a failure.

"The Lakers became the first team in the history of the National Basketball Association to clinch the league championship five days after the Fourth of July," joked George Kiseda of Philadelphia's *Evening Bulletin*.

Wilt, who was thirty-two years old at the start of the season, was used to being the number-one guy on any team. He was still a great talent, but he was no longer an unstoppable force, and the Lakers would continue to revolve around West and Baylor. Adjusting to his new role was difficult for Wilt. He immediately butted heads with Lakers coach Butch van Breda Kolff. The team may have looked flawless on paper, but reality proved to be another matter.

"The bad outweighed the good with [Wilt]," Breda Kolff told biographer Robert Cherry years later. "Wilt was Wilt and had his ego, which was as large as him."

The transition was difficult. The Lakers lost three of their first four games, including a 114–96 defeat to Wilt's old team, the 76ers. Wilt's mind wasn't entirely focused on basketball either. His father wasn't well and died on October 31.

Things didn't improve on the court. Breda Kolff actually benched Wilt for a quarter in one game. In another game, Wilt scored a grand total of two points—unheard of for the most prolific scorer in NBA history. The news wasn't all bad—Wilt also managed games of 60 and 66 points—but the big man wasn't proving to be all Lakers fans had hoped he would be.

Despite all the drama, Wilt and the Lakers finished strong, winning the weak Western Division. Wilt averaged 20.5 points and 21.1 rebounds—good numbers by anyone's standard but Wilt's. Neither San Francisco nor Atlanta posed a real challenge in the playoffs. The Lakers found themselves in a familiar position, facing Boston in the NBA Finals. The series was the sixth time the two franchises had met in the finals, and Boston had won the previous five times. Could the combination of Wilt, West, and Baylor change that trend?

Early on, it looked as if 1969 was finally the Lakers' year. West was dominant in the first two games, scoring 53 and 41 points, and the Lakers jumped out to a 2–0 series lead. No team had ever come back from a 0–2 deficit in the NBA Finals, and the Celtics looked as if they were all but finished. From there, however, the Celtics managed to capture their old magic and won four of the next five games to claim one more NBA title. The comeback was shocking from a team that many considered too old to compete with the Lakers. Wilt ended a close Game 7 on the bench, having injured his knee late in the second half. He had insisted to Breda Kolff that he was okay and could go back in the game. But the coach elected to leave him on the bench, saying he didn't think Wilt would have made a difference anyway.

❝I don't believe [Wilt] is a loser. I believe it's a bad rap against him. I've lost as much as he's lost. . . . People think he's Superman. He's not Superman.❞

—JERRY WEST

Breda Kolff's decision sparked a major controversy. Some suggested Breda Kolff had left Wilt on the bench out of spite, wanting to win the title without relying on the team's best player. Wilt later wrote that the incident left him as angry as he'd ever been at anyone. He felt that his coach had given away a championship.

Breda Kolff, under intense criticism and facing the likelihood of being fired, resigned as coach of the Lakers. Joe Mullaney, a successful college coach, took his place. Mullaney took over a team still considered by many to be the favorite to win the NBA title, and all looked well early in the 1969–1970 season. Wilt was playing better, averaging over 27 points per game, when disaster struck.

On November 7, 1969, the Lakers faced off against the Phoenix Suns. Wilt was having a great game, having made all of his 13 shots. He was adding to his 33 points as he received a pass from West and moved toward the basket. But instead of putting up a shot, Wilt fell to the floor in pain. He had ruptured a tendon and torn a ligament in his knee. Ironically, after all the tough physical abuse Wilt had taken over the years, his first serious injury had come without any contact at all.

Wilt needed surgery to repair the injury. He promised fans that he'd be back soon. But some wondered whether, at Wilt's age, he'd ever be able to come back. His doctors didn't think he'd play again that season. Wilt took that as a challenge. While the Lakers played on, Wilt rehabilitated his knee. He claimed that sometimes he spent 10 hours a day on his rehab. Part of Wilt's therapy included playing volleyball, a sport he thoroughly enjoyed.

Wilt's hard work paid off. He returned to the court that season. On March 18, with just three games left in the regular season, he rejoined the Lakers. He played 23 minutes, scoring 15 points and grabbing 9 rebounds in a Lakers loss.

Without Wilt for most of the season, the Lakers had finished second in the Western Division. But with Wilt back on the team, the Lakers were once again a force. They overcame a 3–1 series deficit to beat the Suns in the first round of the playoffs.

Then they swept the Atlanta Hawks in the division finals. The Lakers advanced to the NBA Finals, and for once, a team other than the Boston Celtics was waiting.

The New York Knicks had enjoyed a fantastic season and had carried that momentum right into the playoffs. In the finals, they used a balanced attack, not allowing the Lakers to focus on any one player defensively. The tactic worked, and the Knicks won the opening game, 124–112. The series was a back-and-forth affair. The Lakers won to tie the series 1–1 and then lost a thrilling overtime game to give the advantage back to New York. Game 4 was another nail-biter, this time with Los Angeles winning in overtime.

In Game 5, the Lakers appeared poised to take over. They had a 13-point halftime lead, and New York's best player, Willis Reed, was on the bench with an injury. But the Knicks kept fighting and used a smothering defense to erase the deficit and stage an unlikely comeback victory.

With Reed still out, the Lakers bounced back to tie the series at 3–3. That set up a winner-take-all Game 7, to be played in New York's Madison Square Garden.

To the delight of his teammates and the home crowd, Reed came onto the court just before tip-off. He didn't play a lot during the game, but his presence was an emotional boost that the Knicks badly needed. The Lakers, meanwhile, looked flat. In the biggest game of the year, they all but mailed it in (including a 1–11 performance from Wilt at the free-throw line). They trailed by 27 at halftime and never posed a threat. The New York fans got to celebrate with their team after a 113–99 victory. Once again, the Lakers had fallen short. After the series, media and fans around the nation praised Reed's courage for returning from an injury. Nobody bothered to mention all that Wilt had done to return from a much more serious physical problem.

GAINING RESPECT

During his years with the Lakers, fans around the NBA seemed to warm to Wilt. For years the crowds at opposing arenas had lustily booed Wilt, but he noted that had changed late in his career. Part of the change might have been that Wilt was no longer such a dominant force on the court, and he no longer made everything look so easy. Wilt himself credited his knee injury—and the work he did to recover from it—as the reason he'd finally started to win over the fans.

Wilt returned healthy for the 1970–1971 season, but the same couldn't be said for some of his teammates. Baylor suffered a leg injury that basically ended his career, and the Lakers also lost West to a knee injury late in the season. That left Wilt to lead the way, which he did with a 20.7 scoring average and a league-high 18.2 rebounds per game. After missing most of the previous season, Wilt played in every game for the Lakers. The team went 48–34 on the year, winning the newly formed Pacific Division. (The Eastern and Western divisions had been expanded into conferences, subdivided into two divisions each.)

The Lakers opened the playoffs against the Chicago Bulls. The series was tight, with each team winning every home game. Fortunately for the Lakers, they had home court advantage as a result of their division title. They won the series four games to three and advanced to the Western Conference Finals.

A new force in the NBA waited for them there—the Milwaukee Bucks. The Bucks were led by superstar guard Oscar Robertson and young, up-and-coming center Lew Alcindor. (Lew Alcindor changed his name to Kareem Abdul-Jabbar during the 1971–1972 NBA season after converting to Islam.) The Bucks had dominated the league, posting a 66–16 record and winning 20 games in a row at one point. Alcindor was the league's leading scorer and MVP. For more than a decade, Chamberlain versus Russell had been the league's premier matchup of big men. Instead, it became Chamberlain versus Alcindor.

In his prime, Wilt would have been a match for the talented Alcindor. Unfortunately for Lakers fans, Wilt was decidedly out of his prime, and it showed. Alcindor and the Bucks dominated the Lakers. Los Angeles managed just one win in the entire series, and in their four losses, Milwaukee blew them out each time. Once again, the Lakers had come up empty in their search for a title.

Wilt wasn't ready to give up the spotlight yet, however. He had a new plan to fight former heavyweight boxing champion Muhammad Ali. The two men were prepared to go through with the fight and even called a press conference to sign the contract. But contract details got in the way, and eventually Wilt thought better of the idea. No one denied that Wilt was strong, but he was no boxer, and Ali could have seriously hurt him. At best, Wilt would have been thoroughly embarrassed before a worldwide audience. The fight never happened.

By the 1971–1972 season, the face of the Lakers was changing. They had a new head coach, former Celtics guard Bill Sharman. Baylor was beyond his prime and retired early in the season, and Wilt's skills were quickly diminishing. West was the team's star, along with young guard Gail Goodrich. Wilt was no longer a big-time scorer, but his defense remained critical to the team's success. Sharman named Wilt captain, calling on his experience for leadership.

The new combination was a huge success. The new-look Lakers were all but unstoppable. On November 5, the team entered a game against the Baltimore Bullets sporting a 6–3 record. The Lakers managed a tight four-point win over the Bullets.

Los Angeles wouldn't lose again for more than two months. With a run-and-gun style, they overwhelmed opponents. Wilt's role was to rebound the ball and quickly outlet (pass) it to one of the guards, who would press it up the court and look for a quick basket. The Lakers built a winning streak that just wouldn't stop. An overtime victory over the Suns on December 10 marked the team's twentieth win in a row.

"A lot of streaks are predicated [based] on luck," Wilt told reporters. "This isn't one of them. We haven't had many close games."

On December 19, against the 76ers, Wilt scored 32 points, snagged 34 rebounds, and blocked 12 shots as the Lakers won their 25th in a row, 154–132. Two games later, they broke the NBA record with 27 wins in a row. The streak soared past 30. A victory over the Cleveland Cavaliers on January 5, 1972, made it 32 in a row. Two nights later, the Lakers dominated the Atlanta Hawks to extend the streak to 33.

The defending NBA champs, the Bucks, finally put an end to the streak on January 9. The tremendous stretch of wins propelled Los Angeles to a record of 69–13—the best regular-season mark in NBA history at the time—and first place in the Pacific Division. The season came with personal milestones for Wilt as well. He overtook Russell as the league's all-time leading rebounder. He also became the first player ever to score 30,000 points in his career. Wilt was still making headlines, even if his scoring average had dipped to a mere 14.8 points per game.

The Lakers' winning ways carried right into the playoffs. They cruised through the first round, sweeping the Chicago Bulls in four games. Then they dispatched the defending champs, the Bucks. Once again, Los Angeles was headed to the NBA Finals. Would 1972 finally be the year they got over the hump and won a title?

The Knicks were waiting. New York jumped out early and handed the Lakers a shocking 114–92 defeat in Los Angeles in the first game. But then Wilt and the Lakers took over. They easily handled New York in Games 2 and 3. Then, in Game 4, the Lakers appeared to be in trouble. In a close game, Wilt picked up his fifth foul late in the fourth quarter. In his thirteen NBA seasons, Wilt had never fouled out of a game, but he was one foul away from doing exactly that. The game went into overtime, and Wilt had to play careful but aggressive defense.

The Lakers scored on the opening possession of the overtime. Then the Knicks went on offense. New York center Jerry Lucas got the ball and drove it toward the basket—and toward Wilt. Wilt spun his body and reached over Lucas's back just as Lucas pulled up for a shot. The play was risky. Even a little contact would have meant a foul. Wilt blocked the shot cleanly, a play that ignited the Lakers and helped them claim a 116–111 victory to move within a game of the championship.

But there was a problem. After the game, Wilt's wrist was swollen and hurting from a fall he'd taken. At first doctors thought the wrist was just sprained. But they later found out it was broken. That didn't stop Wilt, however. He told doctors to give him drugs to take down the swelling. He spent all night icing the wrist. He refused to sit on the bench with a championship so close at hand.

"We brought a ball into the locker room," said the team doctor. "As soon as I saw [Wilt] palm it, catch it, and throw it, I knew enough flexibility had been restored so he could play. But, believe me, this was a serious injury and an unexpectedly fast recovery."

Even with a broken wrist, Wilt was a force on the court for Game 5. He scored 24 points and collected 29 rebounds. More important, his stellar defense made life miserable for the Knicks. By the end, the Lakers had a 114–100 victory and an

NBA championship. Elated Los Angeles fans stormed onto the court and hoisted Wilt—the series MVP—up on their shoulders.

Peter Carry of *Sports Illustrated* wrote: "In the end [Wilt] shut up—perhaps forever—those critics who for years claimed that he was a quitter, that he could not win important games."

Chapter Nine

Life after Basketball

Wilt and the Lakers were on top of the basketball world following their record-setting season and championship in 1972. Wilt used some of the fortune he'd made playing in the NBA to build a mansion in Los Angeles. And already, he was thinking of life after basketball. His thirty-six-year-old body wouldn't hold up to many more bruising seasons in the NBA.

In what would be his final NBA season, Wilt's scoring was further diminished. He averaged just 13.2 points per game. But that does not mean he was ineffective. He led the league in rebounding for the eleventh time. He also set an NBA record that still stands by making 73 percent of the shots he took. Wilt was still a valuable contributor to his team, just in a different way than he had been in his younger years.

The 1972–1973 season was a good one for the Lakers. Once again, they won the Pacific Division and beat Chicago in the first round of the playoffs. Wilt's stellar defense in Game 7 of the series helped the Lakers seal the deal and advance to face the Golden State Warriors in the Western Conference Finals. The Warriors were no match for the Lakers, with Los Angeles winning the series 4–1.

For the third time in four years, the Lakers and Knicks squared off for the title. Jerry West was hampered by a leg injury, and the Lakers couldn't compensate. The Knicks won four games to one to claim the championship.

"The Knicks are so well-balanced, and have tremendous passing and so many good shooters, you can't concentrate on one man," Wilt said after the series. "The key to the series was that their defense stopped our running game." In the final game, Wilt scored 23 points and collected 21 rebounds.

That summer Wilt focused on his newest passion—volleyball. His height, strength, and agility made him a natural for the game. (His age and lack of proper technique prevented him from becoming a truly great player, however.) He toured North America with a traveling team of volleyball stars that would eventually become known as Wilt's Big Dippers.

Volleyball had never been a big attraction in North America, but for a little while, Wilt helped to change that. "All of a sudden, attention was focused on our volleyball team because Wilt was one of the most recognizable athletes in the world," said teammate and volleyball legend Gene Selznick. "Wilt could promote anything. He did more for volleyball than anyone else in the 53 years I've been in [the sport]."

Wilt loved the game. He was not a great all-around player, but he could spike the ball and get the fans excited. And Wilt was having a blast. Those who watched him play said that he never looked as happy on the basketball court as he did while playing with the Big Dippers.

Wilt's basketball future was still in question at this time. The Lakers owned his rights for the 1973–1974 season. But Wilt decided he didn't want to play in the NBA anymore. He wanted to give the upstart ABA a try and signed a contract to be a player-coach for the San Diego Conquistadors (called the Q's for short).

But there was a problem. The Lakers protested, saying that because Wilt's rights were owned by Los Angeles, he could not play professional basketball for anyone else. Rather than give in to the Lakers, Wilt shocked his fans by announcing his retirement as a professional basketball player. He would take the job as San Diego's head coach but would not play.

The Q's were a young, inexperienced team, and Wilt was anything but a typical coach. He knew his shortcomings, however, and left most of the day-to-day coaching to his assistants. Wilt was the coach in name only. He was there more for publicity than anything else. The Q's went 37–47 in Wilt's only season as an ABA head coach. They made the playoffs but were knocked out by the Utah Stars in the first round.

Wilt knew that coaching wasn't for him. He left the Q's in 1974. In October of that year, he wrote an article for *Sports Illustrated* to explain that he was not coming back. "Teams are still competing for me, only now they're offering me figures that are getting to be around a million dollars a year," Wilt wrote. "This time I've decided to turn them all down. I've decided to retire from basketball, as player and as coach. . . . I've taken my last professional shot and I don't even remember whether it went in. It doesn't matter. I changed the whole sport of basketball in many ways—more than people want to give me credit for. But I'm satisfied."

That wasn't to say that thirty-seven-year-old Wilt was stepping out of the public spotlight. He continued to play volleyball—both the organized version and in impromptu beach volleyball sessions. He helped to establish and sponsor a high-level girls' track-and-field team in Los Angeles. He also took up new sporting interests, such as racquetball and tennis. He became a board member of the newly founded International Volleyball Association (IVA) and in 1975 became the IVA president. He helped promote the league and played occasionally over the next five years, until the IVA folded in 1979. Most famously, Wilt was named MVP of the league's 1975 All-Star game. Wilt would later be named to the Volleyball Hall of Fame (more for his promotion of the sport than his playing ability).

WILT'S WONDER WOMEN

Wilt received $5,000 from *Sports Illustrated* for the piece he wrote announcing his retirement. He reportedly used that money to sponsor a girls' track-and-field team called the La Jolla Track Club (the team changed its name to Wilt's Wonder Women in honor of their benefactor). Wilt worked with the girls, helping to mentor the team members. The team's most famous member, Patty Van Wolvelaere, went on to become a two-time Olympian.

Wilt even flirted with a return to the NBA. Rumors swirled that the Knicks wanted him to join their team. But in the end, no deal got done (largely because Wilt was still technically the property of the Lakers). After a mandatory five-year wait after retirement, Wilt was enshrined into the Basketball Hall of Fame in 1979. A huge crowd turned out to watch Wilt's induction.

"Looking back on it," Wilt said in his Hall of Fame speech, "I'm glad I came from Philadelphia. It was a mecca [center] of basketball back then. I feel I wouldn't have been a great basketball player if I hadn't been brought up in Philadelphia."

In 1982—almost a decade after his retirement—Wilt was still being courted by professional teams. The New Jersey Nets wanted him to come out of retirement. Wilt declined, saying that he didn't want to deal with the grueling travel schedule of an NBA player. But he still believed he could compete and said that if he did come back, he'd lead the league in both rebounds and blocked shots.

> **"**My ego is such that I liked it when [an NBA team] said they could use me. . . . Come February, where do you think I'd rather be: in Cleveland trying to plow my way through a snowstorm to get to the game or on a beach in Hawaii, board sailing and chasing girls?**"**
>
> —WILT CHAMBERLAIN, 1984

Wilt had a passion for movies and had long dreamed of producing and acting in them. In the early 1980s, he got his chance to show his stuff on the big screen. He was cast as the villain Bombaata in the 1984 film *Conan the Destroyer*, starring Arnold Schwarzenegger. Wilt didn't have many lines in the movie, and his performance met with poor reviews, but nobody could deny his physical presence on the screen. Regardless, no other movie producers came knocking thereafter. *Conan* was his only movie credit.

In 1984 Kareem Abdul-Jabbar surpassed Wilt's career NBA scoring record of 31,419 points. Wilt wasn't on hand to see his record erased, but he was at a ceremony in Los Angeles to honor Abdul-Jabbar the next day.

Wilt was an avid reader and also tried his hand at writing. In 1991 he released a book titled *A View from Above*. The book wasn't really an autobiography, though it did contain many stories from Wilt's life. The book was more about Wilt's personal philosophy, worldview, and how he coped with his own celebrity. The book stirred up controversy, however. Wilt made some wild claims in the book, especially about his personal life, that offended many people. In 1997 he released another book, *Who's Running the Asylum? Inside the Insane World of Sports Today*. In the book, Wilt discussed the state of modern sports and the direction they were taking. He gave his opinions on everything from the role of money in modern athletics to the secondary status of women's sports.

By the late 1990s, Wilt's health was in decline. He was having heart troubles. They showed up in the form of edema— a buildup of fluid in the body. The fluid collected in Wilt's legs, making them swollen and painful. In early fall 1999, Wilt had root canal surgery on two teeth. The surgery was a failure, and Wilt decided to get tooth implants instead. On October 6, he had the first of several surgeries for the implants. After the surgery, he was in extreme pain—so much that it brought tears to his eyes. Over the next few days, Wilt got weaker. He wasn't eating. He could barely walk.

In 1997 the NBA celebrated its 50th year by naming its 50 all-time greatest players. Wilt was named to the team.

On October 12, Wilt's gardener noticed that he hadn't seen Wilt around the house all day. He went inside and found Wilt lying in his bed, unresponsive. He called 911. Paramedics arrived, but there was nothing they could do. Wilt Chamberlain, sixty-three, was dead. His official cause of death was heart failure.

On the morning of Wilt's Los Angeles funeral, a strong earthquake struck Southern California. At the service, one of the speakers joked that it must have come from one of Wilt's powerful dunks.

Wilt's Legacy

One could argue that no player has ever dominated a major team sport the way Wilt Chamberlain dominated the NBA. Wayne Gretzky did things on ice that no other hockey player could. Babe Ruth almost single-handedly invented the idea of the baseball superstar. Michael Jordan was a dynamic scorer and tenacious defender on the basketball court. But for all the greatness of these players, none could so consistently and thoroughly dominate their competition the way that Wilt could. From the moment he set foot onto the NBA hardwood as a rookie, he was by far the best player in the league. His combination of size, agility, and natural talent may never be matched.

And yet Wilt's legacy remains a matter of debate. For all the physical gifts he possessed, he managed just two NBA championships over his career—a far cry from many of the game's other greats. (Russell had eleven; Jordan had six; Abdul-Jabbar had six; and as of 2009, Shaquille O'Neal had four.) Whether it's fair or not, a player's greatness, in the minds of many, hinges on his success on the biggest stages. Wilt reached the NBA Finals six times and came away empty-handed four of those times. Does that say something about Wilt or merely about the teams he played for?

Further clouding Wilt's status as one of the greatest to play the game was his approach. He was labeled a self-centered player. He was contentious and, in many ways, a coach's worst nightmare. Critics said he relied on his physical talents and squandered his potential by not fully dedicating himself to his craft. These criticisms followed Wilt throughout his career and long after it.

Controversy seemed to follow Wilt wherever he went. Even in retirement, he couldn't avoid it. With his reputation as a selfish player, many people point to him as a representation of what is wrong with sports. But others see him as an example of all that is right.

Basketball allowed Wilt to rise up from his modest upbringing to achieve both fame and wealth. When he was on the basketball court, he worked as hard as anyone, and despite his relative lack of championships, he proved himself a winner (he had only one losing season in his entire career).

He was a player that many people loved to hate. But he was also a player that no opponent wanted to face. His place in NBA history is secure. We will almost certainly never see another player like him.

PERSONAL STATISTICS

Name:

Wilton Norman Chamberlain

Nickname:

The Big Dipper, Wilt the Stilt

Born:

August 21, 1936, in Philadelphia, Pennsylvania

Height:

7 feet 1

Weight:

275 pounds

College:

University of Kansas

Position:

Center

CAREER REGULAR-SEASON STATISTICS

Year	Team	G	FG%	RPG	APG	PPG
1959–1960	PHW	72	.461	27.0	2.3	37.6
1960–1961	PHW	79	.509	27.2	1.9	38.4
1961–1962	PHW	80	.506	25.7	2.4	50.4
1962–1963	SFW	80	.528	24.3	3.4	44.8
1963–1964	SFW	80	.524	22.3	5.0	36.9
1964–1965	TOT	73	.510	22.9	3.4	34.7
1965–1966	PHI	79	.540	24.6	5.2	33.5
1966–1967	PHI	81	.683	24.2	7.8	24.1
1967–1968	PHI	82	.595	23.8	8.6	24.3
1968–1969	LAL	81	.583	21.1	4.5	20.5
1969–1970	LAL	12	.568	18.4	4.1	27.3
1970–1971	LAL	82	.545	18.2	4.3	20.7
1971–1972	LAL	82	.649	19.2	4.0	14.8
1972–1973	LAL	82	.727	18.6	4.5	13.2
Career		1045	.540	22.9	4.4	30.1

Key: **G** = games; **FG%** = field goal percentage; **RPG** = rebounds per game; **APG** = assists per game; **PPG** = points per game

GLOSSARY

draft: a system for selecting new players for professional sports teams

edema: swelling caused by excessive fluid in the body

exhibition: a game played just for show. The game's result does not count toward any official standings.

goaltending: an infraction in which a defensive player touches the ball while it is on its downward arc. Offensive goaltending occurs when an offensive player touches a ball on or above the rim.

pancreas: an organ in the human body that releases hormones and digestive juices

rebound: to collect the ball after a missed shot

rookie: a first-year player

segregation: the practice of having separate public facilities, such as schools and bathrooms, for people of different races

shot put: a track-and-field event in which competitors try to throw a heavy metal ball as far as they can

SOURCES

3 Associated Press, "Wilt: 'I Maybe Could Have Scored 140,'" ESPN. com, October 13, 1999, http://static.espn.go.com/nba/news/1999/1012/110687.html (February 15, 2010).

3 Ibid.

5–6 Ibid.

9 Robert Cherry. *Wilt: Larger Than Life: The Definitive Biography of Wilt Chamberlain* (Chicago: Triumph Books, 2004), 6.

12 Ibid., 30.

12 Ibid., 17.

14 Ibid.

19 Ibid., 48.

21 Tex Maule and Jeremiah Tax, "The Magnetic Obsession," *Sports Illustrated*, March 25, 1957, http://vault.sportsillustrated.cnn.com/vault/article/magazine/MAG1132500/index.htm (February 15, 2010).

21 Ibid.

24 Cherry, *Wilt: Larger Than Life*, 56.

25 Ibid., 45.

30 Jeremiah Tax, "Here Comes the Big Fellow at Last," *Sports Illustrated*, October 26, 1959, http://sportsillustrated.cnn.com/vault/article/magazine/MAG1134161/index.htm (February 15, 2010).

32 Ibid.

34 Cherry, *Wilt: Larger Than Life*, 95.

36 Ibid., 98.

37 Ibid., 95

39 Ibid., 99.

39 Pomerantz, *Wilt*, 1962, 127–128.

40 Ray Cave, "McGuire Raises a Standard," *Sports Illustrated*, October 30, 1961, http://sportsillustrated.cnn.com/vault/article/magazine/MAG1073148/index.htm (February 15, 2010).

41 Ibid.

42 Gary M. Pomerantz, *Wilt, 1962: The Night of 100 Points and the Dawn of a New Era* (New York: Crown Publishers, 2005), 67.

42 Ibid.

44 Associated Press, "Wilt: 'I Maybe Could Have Scored 140'," ESPN. com, October 13, 1999, http://static.espn.go.com/nba/news/1999/1012/110687.html (February 15, 2010).

46 Cherry, *Wilt: Larger Than Life*, 116.

49 Tom C. Brody, "Meet the New Wilt Chamberlain," *Sports Illustrated*, March 2, 1964, http://sportsillustrated.cnn.com/vault/article/magazine/MAG1075691/index.htm (February 15, 2010).

50 Ibid.

50 Wilt Chamberlain and Bob Otto, "I'm Punchy from Basketball, Baby, and Tired of Being a Villain," *Sports Illustrated*, April 12, 1965, http://sportsillustrated.cnn.com/vault/article/magazine/MAG1077071/index.htm (March 15, 2010).

51 Cherry, *Wilt: Larger Than Life*, 85.

51 Ibid., 108.

51 Ibid.

55 Ibid., 138.

56 Ibid., 140.

56 Wilt Chamberlain, "I Love This Game Baby . . . But It Can't Go on This Way," *Sports Illustrated*, April 19, 1965, http://sportsillustrated.cnn.com/vault/article/magazine/MAG1077137/index.htm (February 15, 2010).

57 Mitch Lawrence, "Chamberlain's Feats the Stuff of Legend," ESPN. com, October 15, 1999, http://static.espn.go.com/nba/columns/lawrence_mitch/110858.html (February 15, 2010).

61 Cherry, *Wilt: Larger Than Life*, 162.

62 Ibid., 170.

65 Ibid., 173-174.

65 Frank Deford, "The New Spirit of the 76ers," *Sports Illustrated*, April 17, 1967, http://sportsillustrated.cnn.com/vault/article/magazine/MAG1079750/index.htm (February 15, 2010).

68   Cherry, *Wilt: Larger Than Life*, 178.

70   Ibid., 191.

75   Ibid., 210.

75   Ibid., 213.

77   Ibid., 223.

83   Ibid., 258.

85   Peter Carry, "Swish and They're In," *Sports Illustrated*, May 15, 1972, http://sportsillustrated.cnn .com/vault/article/magazine/ MAG1086089/index.htm (February 15, 2010).

86   Ibid.

88   Darryl Howerton, "In Style," NBA. com, n.d., http://www.nba.com/ encyclopedia/finals/InStyle_1973 .html (February 15, 2010).

88–89   Cherry, *Wilt: Larger Than Life*, 292.

90   Wilt Chamberlain, "My Impact Will Be Everlasting," Sports Illustrated, October 7, 1974, http:// sportsillustrated.cnn.com/vault/ article/magazine/MAG1089076/ index.htm (February 16, 2010).

91   Cherry, *Wilt: Larger Than Life*, 315.

92   Ibid., 316.

BIBLIOGRAPHY

Chamberlain, Wilt. *A View from Above.* New York: Villard
    Books, 1991.

Cherry, Robert. *Wilt: Larger Than Life: The Definitive Biography
    of Wilt Chamberlain.* Chicago: Triumph Books, 2004.

Lynch, Wayne. *Season of the 76ers: The Story of Wilt
    Chamberlain and the 1967 NBA Champion Philadelphia
    76ers.* New York: St. Martins Press, 2002.

Pomerantz, Gary M. *Wilt, 1962: The Night of 100 Points and the
    Dawn of a New Era.* New York: Crown Publishers, 2005.

Taylor, John. *The Rivalry: Bill Russell, Wilt Chamberlain, and the
    Golden Age of Basketball.* New York: Random House, 2005.

WEBSITES

Basketball-Reference.com

http://www.basketball-reference.com

Basketball-Reference.com is packed with NBA statistics. Type Wilt's name into the search box to get almost any statistic imaginable on the star center.

NBA.com

http://www.nba.com

The official site of the NBA has all the latest news, scores, standings, and statistics.

NBA Encyclopedia—Wilt Chamberlain

http://www.nba.com/history/players/chamberlain_summary.html

Visit this page to read a summary of Wilt's career, with stats, honors, and more.

INDEX